Original title:
Witches' Lullaby

Copyright © 2024 Creative Arts Management OÜ
All rights reserved.

Author: Clement Portlander
ISBN HARDBACK: 978-9916-85-159-3
ISBN PAPERBACK: 978-9916-85-160-9

Enchanting Nocturne

In the dead of night, when stars softly gleam,
Whispers of magic enchant in my dream,
Mystical creatures, unseen yet near,
In the silence of darkness, their presence is clear.

Moonlight dances on the edge of the night,
Casting shadows in silver, soft and light,
Swaying to melodies whispered by the wind,
Lost in enchantment, a spell to bind.

Underneath the velvet cloak of the sky,
Where secrets linger and shadows fly,
Echoes of incantations softly croon,
Guiding spirits to the enchanted moon.

Whispers of the night, in the midnight air,
Mysteries unfold, free from the day's stare,
Spirits whisper secrets in a ghostly trance,
Lost in the magic, caught in the dance.

Coven's Harmony

Beneath the moonlit sky,
In the darkened wood, we fly,
Whispers of magic fill the air,
In the coven's embrace, we find solace.

Moonlit Reveries

Moon's gentle glow above,
Guiding us with ancient love,
Lost in dreams of long ago,
Where shadows dance, secrets show.

Shadows' Melody

In the shadows' silent song,
Weaving spells both sweet and strong,
Echoes of the night's soft tune,
Underneath the waning moon.

Spellbound Secrets

Whispers in the dark of night,
Revealing secrets out of sight,
Magic weaves its mystic thread,
In the realm where dreams are fed.

Coven's Dream

In the dead of night, where shadows creep,
Whispers soft, secrets the night doth keep,
Coven gathers, under the moon's gleam,
Swaying in magic, lost in dream.

Veil of Dreams

Beyond the veil where dreams are spun,
Witches dance 'neath the moon and sun,
Singing rhymes of ancient lore,
Weaving spells forevermore.

Song of the Night

Silent whispers in the dark,
Night's magic leaves its mark,
Stars above, the moon's soft light,
Guiding witches through the night.

Moonlit Enchantment

Moonlit path where secrets hide,
Enchantment weaves, the night abide,
Spells are cast in whispered tones,
In the night, the magic moans.

Spellbound Harmonies

Beneath the moonlit sky, shadows dance in tune
Mystical melodies sung by the whispering June
Embracing the enchantment of the night's sweet hum
In spellbound harmonies, the spirits softly thrum

Whispers of the Night

In the silent darkness, the whispers softly sing
Echoes of ancient spells on ethereal wing
Moonlit incantations woven with care
Guiding the lost souls through the midnight air

Magickal Serenade

A magickal serenade lingers in the night
Stars aglow, casting spells with radiant light
Enchanting voices beckon, spirits taking flight
Lost in the symphony of the mystical sight

Stars Aligned

Stars aligned in cosmic harmony above
Weaving magic spells of peace and love
Whispers of the night guide us to the unknown
In the realm of witches, our spirits are sown

Secrets of the Witching Hour

When twilight falls, the magic stirs
Whispers echo from ancient trees
Mysterious secrets the night will bring
Witching hour reveals what's unseen

Whispers in the Shadows

Moonlight dances on whispered breeze
Shadows cloak secrets in the night
Lost incantations softly spoken
In the darkness, magic awoken

Evening Enchantment

The moon's embrace, a mystical sight
Stars align in the velvet sky
Chants of power fill the air
In the evening, magic is everywhere

Mystical Silence

In the hush of the enchanted night
Mystery weaves its silent spell
Whispers of spells carried on the wind
In mystical silence, the witch's power is well

Silent Incantation

Beneath the moon's gentle glow,
Whispers float through the night,
Stars align in a cosmic show,
Magic dances in silent flight.

Mystical Murmur

Shadows twist, the candles gleam,
A mystical murmur fills the air,
Dreams weave through a moonlit stream,
In the witching hour's timeless lair.

Serene Spellcasting

Cauldron bubbles, herbs entwine,
A serene spellcasting atmosphere,
In the stillness of the starlit shrine,
The enchantress weaves her prayer.

Twilight's Ode

Twilight whispers, a velvet cloak,
A symphony of owls softly sings,
In hidden corners, secrets spoke,
Nature's melody takes on mystical wings.

Cauldron Hush

Under moon's soft glow, cauldron's whispers low,
Stirring secrets of the night, an ancient rhythmic flow,
Spells woven in the shadows, where mystic energies brush,
In the witching hour's embrace, a soothing cauldron hush.

Mystic Reverie

In a realm of dreams unseen, where magic holds the key,
Whispers of the stars above, guide the mystic reverie,
A spellbound dance under the moon, where spirits come alive,
In the enchanting night's embrace, where witches thrive.

Nightfall Serenade

Velvet darkness descends as the twilight fades away,
Echoes of enchantment in the shadows start to play,
Moonlit melodies entwine, in a haunting serenade,
Where nocturnal creatures roam and secrets are displayed.

Enigmatic Harmony

In the balance of nature's song, where light and darkness meet,
Whispers of the ancients hum in an enigmatic harmony sweet,
Spellbound souls unite in the mystical midnight air,
Under spells of ancient lore, in the witch's lair.

Hushed Incantations

In the dark of night, shadows dance and sway,
Whispers in the wind, beckoning you to stay,
Underneath the moon, where secrets softly play,
The spell is woven, as dreams come out to play.

Starlit Soothing

Beneath the twinkling stars, a soothing melody,
Guiding you through dreams with celestial harmony,
Close your eyes and drift into the night's serenity,
Magic in the cosmos, embracing you gently.

Shadows' Embrace

In the shadows' arms, find solace and release,
Whispers of enchantment, granting you peace,
Embrace the darkness, where fears and worries cease,
Lost in the night, where mysteries never cease.

Dreamweaver's Song

Through the realm of dreams, the weaver softly sings,
Threads of fantasy woven with delicate wings,
Chasing moonbeams, where imagination springs,
In the dreamweaver's song, the night forever clings.

Midnight Reverie

Underneath the moonlight's glow
Shadows dance in eerie flow
Whispers of magic softly hum
In the midnight's sacred realm

Stars above in tranquil grace
Watchful eyes embrace each space
Dreams take flight on whispered wings
In the quiet of the night

Ancient trees their wisdom keep
Secrets hidden, buried deep
Softly sing their lullabies
In the stillness of the dark

Celestial Cadence

Moonbeams weave a silver thread
Through the night where dreams are spread
Stars align in cosmic dance
Guiding souls with gentle trance

Planets whisper tales untold
Of mysteries in space unfold
Galaxies in timeless sway
Sing a song of night and day

Celestial bodies hold the key
To realms of magic and mystery
In their dance, we find our way
To the realms where spirits play

Whispers of Enchantment

In the forest deep and old
Whispers of enchantment told
Creatures stir in moonlit glen
Chanting spells beyond our ken

Mystic runes in shadows cast
Echoes of the distant past
Magic weaves its ancient spell
In the darkness where we dwell

Silent winds through branches sigh
Carry secrets, mystify
Magic flows in gentle streams
Guiding us through midnight's dreams

Mystic Serenity

Within the silence of the night
Mystic serenity takes flight
Peaceful spirits softly sing
In the realm where dreams take wing

Candles flicker, casting light
Guiding souls through starry night
Whispers of the unseen world
In the mystic depths unfurled

Cauldron bubbling with mystic brew
Unveiling secrets old and new
Magic dances in the air
Enveloping with gentle care

Whispers in the Night

Through the darkness, shadows dance,
Soothing whispers, in a trance,
Moonlight beams, a soft embrace,
In the night, find solace and grace.

Whispers in the Night

Stars above, shining bright,
Secrets whispered in the night,
Magic weaves its ancient spell,
In the dark, all is well.

Midnight Ode

Midnight's song, a melody
Softly sung by shadows, free
Moonlit dreams, the night reveals,
In the silence, the heart heals.

Midnight Ode

Whispers carried on the breeze,
In the night, we find our ease,
Stars above, guiding light,
In the darkness, shining bright.

Spellbound Serenity

Whispers of magic, softly sung,
In the night, the spells are flung,
Serenity in shadows deep,
In the mystical, find peace to keep.

Spellbound Serenity

Moonlit enchantment fills the air,
In the quiet, banish care,
Spellbound by the mystic charm,
In the night, free from harm.

Shadowed Harmony

In the shadows, whispers sing,
Harmony the darkness brings,
Silent night, the world asleep,
In the shadows, secrets keep.

Shadowed Harmony

Moonlight dances with the night,
In the shadowed world, take flight,
Whispers soft, a gentle breeze,
In the darkness, find your ease.

Mystical Hush

Under the moonlit sky, whispers fill the night,
Stars align, casting a spell of delight,
Cauldron bubbles, dreams take flight,
Children drift off in mystical hush.

Spellbound Dreams

In the forest deep, shadows dance,
Magic weaves its spell, entranced,
Creatures hush, in trance they seem,
Into the night, spellbound dreams.

Bewitched Reverie

Moonbeams soft, caress the night,
Whispers of magic, in the starlight,
Dreams entwined with mystery,
Soothing souls in bewitched reverie.

Lunar Lullabies

The moon above, a glowing guide,
In the dark, it softly confide,
Stars twinkle in the velvet skies,
Sung to sleep by lunar lullabies.

Mystical Lull

In shadows deep, where whispers dwell,
Moonlight dances, a magic spell,
Stars above, their secrets keep,
In dreams, the night will softly swell.

Among the stars, where spirits glide,
Softly hums the night-time tide,
Close your eyes, release your fears,
Guided by the moon, the stars will guide.

Whispers of the ancient boughs,
Embrace the night, beneath the shrouds,
Hear the echoes of the past,
In the darkness, find your peace endowed.

Twilight Spell

In the realm where shadows play,
Twilight falls at close of day,
Whispers carried on the breeze,
A spell is cast in night's embrace.

Through the mist and moonlit haze,
Enchantment weaves its gentle ways,
Stars above, a silent choir,
In twilight's hold, magic stays.

Spectral whispers in the air,
Softly singing everywhere,
Close your eyes and drift away,
In twilight's spell, find solace there.

Ethereal Chant

Ethereal voices softly sing,
In the night, an ancient ring,
Lost in time, a whispered tale,
Through the starlit void they bring.

Underneath the crescent moon,
Echoes of a mystic tune,
In the darkness, shadows play,
Listen to the night's soft croon.

Magical dreams and visions fly,
Through the midnight velvet sky,
Close your eyes and hear the call,
In the ethereal chant, soar high.

Cerulean Silence

Beneath the cerulean skies,
Where the quiet moonlight lies,
Silent whispers fill the air,
In the stillness, spirits rise.

Shadows dance in moon's soft glow,
Secrets from the past bestow,
Calmness cloaked in starlit veil,
Embrace the silence, let it flow.

Whispers fade into the night,
Cloaked in velvet, out of sight,
In the cerulean hush,
Find your peace in shadows light.

Daughters of the Moon

In the silver glow of night's embrace,
Moonbeams dance upon their face,
Mysteries whispered on the wind,
Within their power, secrets pinned.

Shadows weave a path of grace,
As they move with silent pace,
Ancient chants in whispered tune,
Daughters of the moon commune.

Stars above in silent choir,
Guide their spirits, lift them higher,
Guardian spirits, shadows loom,
Watching o'er the moon's bright bloom.

Lunar Lullaby

Under moonlit skies, they sway,
In the night where shadows play,
Softly sing a lullaby,
Stars above, they hear their cry.

Whispers carried on the breeze,
Magical words that gently ease,
Moon's caress, a soothing balm,
In their world of tranquil calm.

Dreams alight on silver beams,
Guiding through the realm of dreams,
Guardians of the night, they keep,
In the lullaby of sleep.

Dark Enchantment

Bathed in shadows, cloaked in night,
Mystic aura, dark delight,
Spells woven in the midnight air,
In their eyes, a distant stare.

In the cauldron of the dark,
Whispers echo, hushed and stark,
Magic weaves its ancient thread,
In the paths where dreams are led.

Through the veil of darkened skies,
Their enchantment never dies,
Bewitched by the night's own song,
In the realm where they belong.

Night Song Ritual

Midnight melodies they chant,
In the forest, shadows grant,
Ancient words of power ring,
In the night, their voices sing.

Circles drawn in moonlit dew,
Stars above bear witness true,
Incantations softly spoken,
Night's embrace, their spirits woken.

A dance beneath the silver light,
In the heart of darkest night,
Ritual of secrets deep,
In the night, their vows they keep.

Witch's Rest

Under the moon's gentle glow,
In the shadows where secrets grow,
She finds solace in the night's caress,
Drifting into a deep, dream-filled mess.

Whispers of magic fill the air,
As she weaves spells with utmost care,
Her tired eyes flutter closed,
Into the abyss of sleep, she softly flows.

Stars above her keep watch,
As the witch's dreams stretch and botch,
In her realm of enchanting dreams,
Guided by moonlight's silver beams.

Lunar Pathway

Moonbeams dance on the forest floor,
Leading the way to the witch's door,
Through the mystic midnight haze,
Into the realm where enchantment sways.

Shadows whisper tales untold,
As the lunar pathway unfolds,
Guiding wanders to the hidden place,
Where magic lingers with grace.

Stars twinkle in the night sky,
As the witch's spirits fly high,
On the lunar pathway she roams,
Where dreams are born in silent domes.

Enchanted Hush

In the hush of the mystical night,
Where the witch finds her respite,
Silence wraps around her tight,
Embracing her in the enchanted light.

Whispers of ancient spells speak low,
As the enchanted hush starts to grow,
Nature's symphony in a lullaby,
Guiding the witch to realms up high.

Moon's silver glow illuminates her face,
In the stillness, she finds her grace,
Lost in dreams of magic's allure,
In the enchanted hush, she feels secure.

Night's Melody

In the velvet cloak of night's embrace,
The witch finds solace in this place,
Where the stars sing a silent melody,
Guiding her to the realm of fantasy.

Whispers of shadows in the dark,
Dance with moonbeams like a spark,
Night's melody plays in her ear,
A symphony of magic drawing near.

Mystical creatures in the night,
Join the witch in her flight,
Through the sky they soar and glide,
In night's melody, they find their stride.

Veil of Tranquility

Beneath the crescent moon's soft glow,
A world of magic begins to show,
Whispers of spells in the night's serene air,
Embracing hearts with a mystical flair.

Cauldrons bubbling with dreams untold,
As stars above their mysteries unfold,
In the silence of the enchanted night,
Peaceful slumber takes its flight.

Mystic realms awaken in the mind,
Where fantasy and reality entwined,
Through the veil of tranquility's mist,
Lost in dreams, we quietly exist.

Enchantment's Embrace

Moonlit shadows dance and sway,
In the realm where enchantments play,
Whispers of magic in the darkened wood,
Entwine our spirits as they should.

In the twilight's enchanting sight,
Stars above with their soft light,
Guiding souls to a mystical place,
Embraced by enchantment's grace.

Spellbound hearts in the hush of night,
In the whispers of the moon's soft light,
Lost in a world of dreams so sweet,
Enchantment's embrace, a lullaby complete.

Midnight Reverie

Midnight whispers in the cool night air,
Echoes of magic everywhere,
Dreams unfurl in the shadow's keep,
Guiding hearts to the realm of sleep.

In the silence of the witching hour,
Moonlit dreams begin to flower,
Lost in a trance of reverie deep,
Where secrets of the night softly creep.

Stars above in their gentle gaze,
Watching over the dreamer's maze,
In the midnight's mystical song,
Sleeping souls peacefully belong.

Arcane Slumber

In the chamber of spells and charms,
Rests a soul in the sorcerer's arms,
Whispers of power in the candle's glow,
Guiding dreams where mysteries flow.

Under the cloak of the mystic night,
Shadows dance in the dim moonlight,
A veil of magic softly weaves,
Quietly lulling all to arcane sleeps.

Through the realms of the unknown,
Echoes of ancient spells intone,
Sorcery's embrace in the night's embrace,
Into the depths of arcane slumber's grace.

Nightfall Whisperings

As twilight falls, the world turns still,
Secrets whispered in the dark chill,
Shadows dance beneath the moon's soft glow,
Whispers of magic as the night's spell unfolds.

Bats take flight on silent wings,
Ghostly voices in the night sing,
Stars above in their silent chorus,
Whispering secrets of ancient forests.

Moonlight bathes the world in silver sheen,
Nightfall whispers of things unseen,
Mysteries veiled in the cloak of night,
Whisperings of enchantment, a magical sight.

Moonlit Reverie

Under the moon's gentle light,
Whispers of spells take flight,
In dreams where shadows play,
Witches' magic holds sway.

Moonbeams weave a mystical tale,
In the night, the spirits wail,
Lost in moonlit reverie,
Drifting into the realm of mystery.

Stars above twinkle and gleam,
Night sky a mesmerizing dream,
Witches' whispers in the breeze,
Moonlit reverie, a world at ease.

Shadow's Serenade

In the realm where shadows sleep,
Whispers of dark secrets keep,
As night descends with velvet ease,
The shadow's serenade begins to tease.

Whispers float on whispered breath,
Darkness weaves its ancient web,
Echoes of spells cast long ago,
In the shadow's serenade that softly flows.

Moonlight filters through the night,
Casting shadows in the pale moonlight,
Whispers linger in the dark,
Shadow's serenade leaves its mark.

Spellbound Whispers

In the silence of the witching hour,
Spellbound whispers hold their power,
Secrets woven in a tapestry of night,
Whispers of magic taking flight.

Candles flicker, casting their glow,
Whispers of spells from long ago,
In the dark where shadows play,
Spellbound whispers guide the way.

Mysteries hidden in the night's embrace,
Whispers of spells in starlit grace,
In the realm where magic stirs,
Spellbound whispers, the enchantment lures.

Spellbound Slumber

In the whispering night so deep,
Gather 'round for dreams to keep,
Stars above and spirits near,
Guiding us to sleep without fear.

Moonlit dances in shadows' keep,
Soft enchantments as we drift and leap,
Underneath a spell's sweet sheen,
Into the realm of dreams unseen.

Secrets whispered, hush, don't stray,
Through the darkness where we play,
Close your eyes, let go, surrender,
To the magic of our spellbound slumber.

Midnight Chant

Echoes of the midnight hour,
Whispers woven in dark power,
Chanting low, in moon's soft light,
Summoning dreams into the night.

Mystic runes and ancient lore,
Weave a web forevermore,
Spirits dance in shadows' shade,
In the mystic night they parade.

Whispers carried on the breeze,
Hush now, listen, with ease,
Voices of the night entwine,
In a midnight chant, divine.

Shadows' Song

In the echoes of the night,
Shadows dance in pale moonlight,
Whispers on the breath of trees,
Sing a haunting symphony.

Mists of magic, dark and deep,
Secrets that the shadows keep,
Lost within their silent rhyme,
A lullaby of shadows' prime.

Mystery in every note,
From the darkness, music float,
Close your eyes and sway along,
To the shadows' haunting song.

Sorcerer's Dream

In the sorcerer's mystic vision,
Cast in shadows, a dream's incision,
Whispers of a spell so deep,
Into the realm where dark dreams sleep.

In the cauldron, brew and weave,
Chant the words, the magic receive,
Dancing spirits in the night,
In the sorcerer's dream, take flight.

Visions of the ancient past,
In the sorcerer's dream, they last,
In the shadowed realm they gleam,
In the sorcerer's wistful dream.

Bewitched Rest

Under silver moon's soft glow,
Whispers in the dark below,
Dreams take flight where shadows play,
Guiding you to realms far away.

Stars twinkle in the midnight sky,
Spirits whisper as time goes by,
Rocking you in a cradle of dreams,
Peaceful slumber, or so it seems.

In the cauldron of the night,
Where shadows dance in the moon's light,
Sleep comes gentle, a comforting nest,
Embraced by magic, in bewitched rest.

Shadow Dance Symphony

Silent shadows weave and sway,
In the twilight, they gently play,
Soft echoes of a mysterious song,
Guiding you where dreams belong.

Moonbeams dance in the night,
Casting illusions, weaving slight,
A symphony of shadows deep,
Lulling you, as you sink in sleep.

Darkness cloaks like a velvet shroud,
Whispers soft like a misty cloud,
In the arms of shadows' embrace,
You find solace, in the quiet space.

Celestial Whispers

Celestial whispers in the air,
Guiding you with tender care,
Through realms of dreams, you softly glide,
In the stillness, secrets reside.

Starlight whispers tales untold,
Secrets of the cosmic fold,
Unveiling mysteries of the night,
In the embrace of lunar light.

Soft breezes carry dreams aloft,
As constellations whisper soft,
Across the sky, a cosmic dance,
Guiding you to a dreamlike trance.

Chalice of Dreams

In the chalice of dreams, you sip and savour,
Visions dance like whispers of favour,
Glistening with moonlit beams divine,
A potion of dreams, pure and fine.

Elixir of slumber, sweet and deep,
In the chalice of dreams, you gently steep,
Drifting in a soothing embrace,
Lost in the magic of a dreamlike place.

Sip from the cup of celestial brew,
Where fantasy blends with what is true,
In the chalice of dreams, where spirits roam,
You find solace, in the night's dark dome.

Night's Alchemy

In shadows deep, where secrets keep,
Whispers dance and spirits leap.
Moonlight weaves its silver thread,
Through the night, our dreams are fed.

Mysteries stir, in the mystic air,
Magic blooms without a care.
Stars above, their watchful eyes,
Witness to our ancient ties.

A witch's song in the midnight air,
Softly sung with tender care.
Guiding souls through velvet night,
In the dark, we find our light.

Mystical Rhapsody

Deep in the woods, where shadows play,
Mystic whispers lead the way.
Whispers of spells in ancient tongue,
Hear the magic, sweetly sung.

Moonlit dance, a mystical sight,
Stars above, casting their light.
Spirits gather 'neath the moon,
Sung into a soft croon.

Enchanting melody fills the air,
Mystical rhapsody, beyond compare.
Lost in the spell of the night,
Guided by the moon's soft light.

Moonlit Whispers

Moonlit whispers in the breeze,
Softly sung among the trees.
Magic dances in the night,
Filling shadows with delight.

Silver beams caress the earth,
Cloaking secrets of rebirth.
Casting spells with whispered words,
In the night, our hearts are stirred.

Stars above, so bright and clear,
Their ancient wisdom drawing near.
Guiding us through darkened skies,
In the moonlit whispers, we see through lies.

Enchanted Vigil

Underneath the starry sky,
Witches' spirits soar up high.
Guardians of the night we keep,
While the world is fast asleep.

Magic flows within our veins,
Whispering secrets to the plains.
Eyes aglow with ancient power,
Watching over midnight hour.

In the silence of the night,
Our enchantments take to flight.
Protecting those who cannot see,
Enchanted vigil, we'll always be.

Nightfall Spell

As shadows dance beneath the moon,
Whispers of magic softly croon,
In darkness deep, the night's soft spell,
A secret realm where dreams do dwell.

Mysteries woven in twilight haze,
Through velvet skies, enchantments blaze,
With gentle touch, the stars align,
In sacred silence, powers entwine.

The world at rest in midnight's keep,
Where mystic forces softly sweep,
In dreams we find our spirits soar,
Nightfall's spell forevermore.

Whispered Dreams

In the hush of the night's embrace,
Whispered dreams weave a fragile lace,
A sorceress' thoughts in shadows deep,
Into the realm of the mystic's sleep.

Soft chants carried on the wind's caress,
A dance of magic, a sweet unrest,
Visions flicker in the candle's glow,
In twilight's realm, we're lost below.

Moonlight beams on the forest's floor,
The ancient trees their secrets store,
A world unseen by mortal eyes,
Where whispered dreams take us to the skies.

Sorceress' Slumber

In a chamber of darkness, the sorceress lies,
Enveloped in dreams as starlight dies,
Her spirit floats in the midnight air,
Lost in realms of forgotten affair.

Through veils of time and shadows deep,
Echoes of power in slumbering sleep,
Her mind a tapestry of spells untold,
In the silence, her secrets unfold.

Her dreams a garden of magic and might,
Where visions dance in the pale moonlight,
In the sorceress' slumber, the world is spun,
A tapestry of enchantments begun.

Ritual of Silence

In the heart of night, a ritual starts,
In whispered silence and ancient arts,
Candles flicker in the sacred space,
Where time and reality embrace.

The sorceress' hands move with grace,
Tracing symbols in the air's embrace,
Incantations rise on the silent air,
In a dance of magic beyond compare.

In the depths of the night, shadows wane,
As the sorceress calls upon the arcane,
A ritual of silence, power untold,
In the whispers of magic, her secrets unfold.

Nocturnal Bliss

Underneath the moon's soft glow,
In the shadows, dreams do grow,
Stars above, in the night's abyss,
Whispers of magic, fill the night with bliss.

In the darkness, secrets hide,
Hear the wind sing, soft and wide,
Whispers of spells, in the cool night air,
A mystical dance, beyond compare.

As the night deepens, the world slows down,
Whispers of enchantment all around,
Sleep, my dear, in tranquility's kiss,
Embraced by the nocturnal bliss.

Enchanted Reverie

In the realm of dreams, where fantasies reside,
Cloaked in mystery, where enchantments glide,
Fairies dance on moonlit strands,
In the enchanted reverie of far-off lands.

Whispers of spells weave through the night,
Guiding you through starry light,
Magic whispers in the wind's soft sigh,
As dreams take flight and reach the sky.

Lost in a world of mystical trance,
Where shadows waltz in a cosmic dance,
Embrace the night, let visions unfold,
In an enchanted reverie, where stories are told.

Starlit Whispers

Beneath the canopy of the velvet night,
Starlit whispers, shimmering bright,
Echoing through the silent air,
A haunting melody beyond compare.

Moonbeams play on the silver stream,
Secrets whispered in a celestial dream,
Stars above, in their silent dance,
Guiding you into a timeless trance.

In the stillness of the midnight hours,
Weaving magic with unseen powers,
Listen closely to the whispers' call,
Embracing the night's enchanting thrall.

Dreamweaver's Chant

In the realm where dreams are spun,
By the whispering breezes, one by one,
Threads of starlight, woven with care,
By the dreamweaver with fiery hair.

Softly humming a mystical tune,
Underneath the glowing moon,
Crafting visions of wonder and delight,
In the dreamweaver's chant, all is right.

Through the realm of twilight's gleam,
Where reality and fantasy stream,
The dreamweaver's chant weaves its spell,
Guiding you through dreams where magic dwells.

Milton Keynes UK
Ingram Content Group UK Ltd.
UKHW022139310524
443357UK00004B/96

9 789916 851593